KONYA

TRAVEL GUIDE

2024

The Sufi Soul of Konya: Mystical Encounters in the City of Rumi

Philip Mablood

TABLE OF CONTENTS

Introduction
    Welcome to Konya
    Geographical Location of konya
    A Brief History of Konya
    Understanding Sufism: The Spiritual
    Essence of Konya
Chapter 1: Exploring Rumi's Legacy
    The Life and Teachings of Rumi
    Rumi's Mausoleum (Mevlana Museum):
    A Pilgrimage Site for Seekers
    Sema Ceremony: Experiencing the
    Whirling Dervishes
Chapter 2: Iconic Landmarks and Historical
Sites
    Alaeddin Mosque and Konya Citadel
    Karatay Madrasa: A Jewel of Seljuk
    Architecture
    Ince Minaret Medrese: Witness to
    Konya's Cultural Heritage
    Konya Archaeological Museum:
    Unveiling Ancient Treasures
Chapter 3: Immersing in Sufi Culture
    Visiting Sufi Tekkes and Zawiyas:

Sanctuaries of Spiritual Practice

Meeting with Modern Sufi Practitioners

Sufi Music and Poetry: Delving into the Soulful Traditions of Konya

Chapter 4: Culinary Delights and Local Flavors

Exploring Konya's Traditional Cuisine: From Mevlana Kebab to Etli Ekmek

Tea Gardens and Turkish Delights: Sampling Konya's Sweet Side

Culinary Workshops and Food Tours: A Tasty Adventure Awaits

Chapter 5: Off the Beaten Path

Day Trips from Konya: Discovering Nearby Gems

Rural Konya: Experiencing Village Life and Rural Hospitality

Eco-Tourism Initiatives: Connecting with Nature in Konya's Surroundings

Chapter 6: Practical Information

Getting to Konya: Transportation Options

Where to Stay: Accommodation Recommendations

Essential Tips for Travelers: Cultural

Etiquette and Safety Guidelines

Conclusion

Embracing the Sufi Soul of Konya: Reflections on a Mystical Journey

Appendix

Glossary of Sufi Terms

Useful Phrases in Turkish

Final Thoughts and Recommendations for Saying Goodbye to Konya

Introduction

Welcome to Konya

Welcome to Konya: A Timeless Journey into Turkey's Spiritual Heart

Conya, a hidden gem in Turkey's Anatolian region, beckons tourists with an abundance of spirituality, culture, and historical significance. This quaint city instantly gives you the impression that time has stood still, with its bustling bazaars, old mosques, and meandering streets all perfectly blending to create a perfect tango between the past and present.

A City of Spiritual Awakening:

Beyond its natural beauty, Konya is alluring due to an otherworldly spiritual energy that permeates the entire city. Mevlana Jalaluddin Rumi, the well-known Sufi mystic, poet, and philosopher, left behind a legacy that has made Konya, popularly referred to as the "City of Rumi," a special place in the hearts of travelers and searchers everywhere.

Journeying into the Heart of Sufism:

For centuries, Konya has been a hub of Sufi wisdom and enlightenment, attracting adherents seeking to penetrate the mysteries of the soul and engage in spiritual dialogue with the Divine. The teachings of Rumi and his followers have had a significant impact on the city's culture, art, and way of life.

Exploring Konya's Spiritual Treasures:

Your journey begins in the Mevlana Museum, which is both a spiritual sanctuary and Rumi's final resting place. Here, surrounded by the exquisite architecture of the museum complex and tranquil gardens, you can pay tribute to the revered poet-saint, immerse yourself in Sufi teachings, and witness the ancient traditions of the Mevlevi Order, which include the fascinating Sema ceremony.

A Tapestry of Cultural Heritage:

Beyond its religious importance, Konya possesses a rich cultural history that begs to be discovered. Discover the winding streets of this ancient town, home to hundreds of years-old mosques, madrasas, and caravanserais that attest to Konya's rich past as a center of Islamic scholarship and trade.

Culinary Delights and Turkish Hospitality:

It wouldn't be a trip to Konya without sampling its delicious food and experiencing the friendly Turkish hospitality. Savor the delectable pastries, fragrant pilafs, juicy kebabs, and flavorful mezes that make up traditional Anatolian cuisine. Try some hot Turkish tea or delectable Turkish coffee as well; these gestures of welcoming eloquently encapsulate the character of Konya's cozy embrace.

A Gateway to Natural Beauty:

Konya's spiritual and cultural attractions are fascinating, but the city also serves as a gateway to the breathtaking natural beauty of the Anatolian plateau. Discover what's outside the city limits: beautiful lakes, verdant valleys, and towering mountains. You may hike, go birdwatching in Sultan Marshes National Park, or just unwind in the peaceful surroundings here.

Embracing the Sufi Soul of Konya:

As you stroll through the city, let yourself be taken away by Konya's Sufi soul—a soul that connects the heart and soul and joins the past, present, earth, and sky. Allow the changing power of spiritual thought, the serenity of Sufi music, and the wisdom of Rumi's poetry to enter your heart.

Welcome to Konya, where the spirit of Rumi and the essence of Sufism thrive around every corner, inviting you to embark on a journey toward self-discovery, inner peace, and enlightenment. Konya welcomes all travelers, pilgrims, seekers, or just curious souls, willing to share its timeless mysteries and let you discover the magnificence of the sacred.

Geographical Location of konya

A Jewel in Turkey's Heartland
Konya, which is located in the center of the Anatolian plateau in Turkey, has a unique geographic position that has influenced its history, culture, and identity for millennia. Konya, which is surrounded by wide plains, undulating hills, and far-off mountain ranges, is a

city of contrasts where old customs and contemporary goals coexist peacefully.

Central Anatolian Plateau:

The Central Anatolian region of Turkey, which covers a sizable portion of the interior of the nation, is where Konya is situated. The Anatolian plateau is bounded to the north by the Taurus Mountains, to the south by the Pontic Mountains, and to the west by the Aegean and Mediterranean Seas. It is distinguished by its high height and level topography.

Strategic Crossroads:

Konya has historically been a center of trade, culture, and civilization due to its strategic location at the intersection of the east, west, and north. Konya, which is located along historic trade routes like the Silk Road and the Spice Route, has been influenced by a wide range of cultures, fusing European, Anatolian,

Persian, and Arabic customs into a singular fabric of history and culture.

Climate and Landscape:

Konya's geographic location affects both its climate and terrain, resulting in an area of extremes with scorching summers, chilly winters, and little precipitation. The city has a continental climate, meaning that summers are hot and dry and winters are cold and snowy. The expansive plains, lush valleys, and sporadic salt lakes that characterize the surrounding terrain offer the city's metropolitan center a striking yet striking backdrop.

Agricultural Heartland:

Konya's rich soil and abundant agricultural output have earned it the nickname "breadbasket of Turkey," despite the region's dry environment. In addition to its booming dairy business, the region is well-known for cultivating a variety of crops, including wheat, barley, and lentils. Konya's position as a center of agricultural expertise is bolstered by the integration of contemporary agricultural techniques with traditional farming methods, which support the local economy.

Natural Wonders:

Beyond its city limits, Konya is encircled by breathtaking natural features that beg to be discovered. The Anatolian plateau's expansive plains extend as far as the eye can see to the east, while the Taurus Mountains to the west provide chances for trekking, skiing, and adventure sports. The bizarre Cappadocia landscapes, the serene Beyşehir Lake, and the historic Catalhoyuk ruins are just a few of the nearby sites that offer countless chances for outdoor play and discovery.

Konya is a city of great significance and timeless beauty because of how its physical location at the intersection of

Anatolia has affected its history, culture, and scenery. The timeless allure of Turkey's heartland may be discovered in Konya, which continues to enthrall guests with its rich legacy, natural beauty, and friendly hospitality. Konya's strategic importance as a hub of trade and commerce stems from its central position on the Anatolian plateau.

A Brief History of Konya

Central Anatolia's Konya has a long and varied history that dates back thousands of years. The city was once called Iconium, and people had lived there since the Neolithic era. It gained notoriety between 1600 and 1200 BCE during the Hittite Empire, and under the Phrygians, Lydians, and Persians, it developed into an important settlement. Before coming under Roman authority in the second century BCE, Konya was a part of the Seleucid Empire in the third century BCE. It thrived as a significant trading hub along the Silk Road, which connected East and West, throughout the Roman era.

Islam's influence in the region began when Arab Muslims captured Konya in the seventh century CE. Later, in the eleventh century, it emerged as a major city within the Seljuk Sultanate of Rum, and in the thirteenth century, under Sultan Alaeddin Keykubad I, it achieved its pinnacle as the capital of the Seljuk Empire. Konya flourished as a hub of Islamic knowledge, art, and culture throughout this time.

The 13th-century arrival of Rumi, also called Mevlana, a well-known Persian poet and mystic, in Konya helped to shape the spiritual and cultural character of the city. People throughout are still motivated by his teachings on spiritual development, love, and tolerance.

Konya was ruled by several Turkic Beyliks following the fall of the Seljuk Empire, and then by the Ottoman Empire in the fifteenth century. Konya maintained its prominence as a hub of Islamic scholarship and culture during the Ottoman era.

Konya has maintained its rich historical and cultural legacy while developing into a thriving metropolis in the modern period. It is today well-known for its Sufi customs, ancient sites, and friendly people, drawing tourists from all over the world to enjoy its ethereal charm.

Understanding Sufism: The Spiritual Essence of Konya

The mystical branch of Islam known as Sufism has had a significant impact on Konya's spiritual and cultural landscape. In this place, Sufism permeates every facet of society and is more than just a belief system.

Origins and Principles:

. Discover the history of Sufism and its core values of compassion, love, and introspection.

. Explore the teachings of well-known Sufi masters, such as Rumi, whose poetry and philosophy still serve as an inspiration to searchers all over the world.

Sufi Orders in Konya:

. Learn about the numerous Sufi organizations (Tariqas) that have flourished in Konya throughout the ages, each with its own traditions and spiritual heritage.

. Discover the fascinating Sema ceremony performed by the renowned Whirling Dervishes of the Mevlevi Order, which was established by Rumi as a means of fostering spiritual devotion.

Sufi Rituals and Practices:

. Learn about the mystical rites and customs followed by Sufis in Konya, such as sama (spiritual music and dancing) and dhikr (remembrance of God).

. Discover the transformative power of Sufi meditation and contemplation for yourself in the tranquil surroundings of Konya's dergahs (spiritual retreats) and tekkes (Sufi lodges).

Sufism in Contemporary Konya:

. Discover how the spiritual legacy of their ancestors is being preserved and transmitted by Sufi masters and practitioners in Konya today, as Sufism continues to flourish there.

. To gain a deeper knowledge of Konya's ongoing spiritual core, interact with the local Sufi groups and take part in spiritual gatherings and Sufi-inspired cultural activities.

Ponder the timeless wisdom of Sufi teachings in managing the complexity of the modern world, as well as the profound influence of Sufism on Konya's personality and spirit.

Chapter 1: Exploring Rumi's Legacy

The Life and Teachings of Rumi

. Explore the life of Jalal ad-Din Muhammad Rumi, also referred to as Rumi, starting with his birth in Balkh, which is now in Afghanistan, and ending with his ultimate relocation to Konya, Turkey.

. Examine the early events that influenced Rumi's spiritual development, particularly his interactions with scholars and spiritual mentors like Shams-i Tabrizi.

Rumi's Teachings:

. Explore the key themes of Rumi's teachings, which include love, harmony, and the quest for enlightenment.

. Examine Rumi's poetry, especially the "Mathnawi," considered to be his greatest and a fount of mystical and spiritual knowledge.

The Concept of Divine Love:

. Examine Rumi's profound interpretation of divine love (ishq), which he saw as the ultimate route to connection with the Divine and the power underlying all reality.

. Consider Rumi's well-known metaphors and allegories, which eloquently describe how love can transcend physical constraints.

Whirling Dervishes and the Sema Ceremony:

. Discover how Rumi founded the Mevlevi Order and the spiritual practices of the Whirling Dervishes, who embody intense devotion via the enthralling Sema ceremony.

. Examine the symbolism found in the Sema ceremony; it symbolizes the soul's path toward enlightenment and oneness with the Divine Beloved.

Legacy and Influence:

. Because Rumi's teachings are still relevant to individuals from all walks of life, consider his lasting influence and global reach.

. Discover how Rumi's poetry and ideas have spread far beyond Konya, inspiring many others to pursue enlightenment and truth in their spiritual quests.

Rumi's Mausoleum (Mevlana Museum): A Pilgrimage Site for Seekers

History of Rumi's Mausoleum:

. Learn about the background of the renowned Mevlana Museum, which is home to the mausoleum of Mevlana, also known as Jalal ad-Din Muhammad Rumi.

. Discover how the location changed from a modest dervish lodge to a well-known destination for pilgrims looking for inspiration and spiritual guidance.

Architecture and Design:

. Examine the mausoleum of Rumi, which is known for its unique Seljuk and Ottoman architectural features.

. Admire the exquisite calligraphy, geometric designs, and tilework that adorn the interior, which showcases the intricacy and beauty of Islamic art and craftsmanship.

The Sacred Shrine of Mevlana:

. Discover the somber ambiance of Rumi's last resting place, where people gather to pay their respects and find comfort in his company from all over the world.

. Consider the shrine's spiritual significance as a site of pilgrimage and prayer where followers of Mevlana converse with his soul and ask for favors to attain spiritual enlightenment and direction.

Exhibits and Artifacts:

. Discover the wealth of antiques, manuscripts, and items about Rumi's life and teachings in the museum.

. Admire exquisite items from the Mevlevi Order, illuminated Qurans, and rare manuscripts of Rumi's poetry that provide insights into the Sufi traditions and rich cultural legacy of Konya.

Whirling Dervishes Ceremony:

. Take in a captivating show by the Whirling Dervishes, which takes place regularly at the museum complex.

. Watch the dervishes' beautiful movements as they swirl in ecstatic devotion, representing the soul's mystical journey toward unity with the Divine.

Spiritual Contemplation and Reflection:

. Settle in for a period of introspection and quiet thought in the serene grounds that encircle Rumi's tomb.

. Take in the calm atmosphere of the hallowed location and let Mevlana's teachings sink into your heart and spirit.

Sema Ceremony: Experiencing the Whirling Dervishes

The Spiritual Significance of the Sema Ceremony:

. Discover the deep spiritual meaning and symbolism of the Sema ceremony, an enthralling ritual carried out by the Mevlevi Order's Whirling Dervishes.

. Learn how the dervishes' circular motions symbolize the cosmic dance of creation and the soul's journey toward unity with the Divine.

Preparation and Ritual:

. Learn about the intense training and spiritual preparation that dervishes undergo to be ready for the Sema ceremony.

. Discover how the whirling is accompanied by complex choreography and rhythmic music that creates a captivating atmosphere that is ideal for spiritual transcendence.

The Whirling Dance:

. Watch the Whirling Dervishes whirl in a moment of blissful surrender, their movements fluid and coordinated.

. Admire the dervishes' ability to stay perfectly balanced and graceful while sensing the universe's divine rhythm.

The Journey of Transformation:

. The dance of the Whirling Dervishes represents the soul's journey from egoism and worldly attachment to spiritual enlightenment and unity with

God. Consider the deeper significance behind this dance.

. Feel a deep sense of inspiration and wonder as you see the dervishes give themselves over to the divine will, overcoming their physical limitations and reaching a state of spiritual bliss.

Participation and Engagement:

. Whether you participate in the Sema ceremony or watch it as an observer, let the ritual's beauty and spirituality enchant you.

. Take advantage of this chance to commune with the ancient wisdom and universal truths that the Whirling Dervishes' dance conveys, which will inspire a fresh sense of wonder and reverence for the holy secrets of life.

Chapter 2: Iconic Landmarks and Historical Sites

Alaeddin Mosque and Konya Citadel

Alaeddin Mosque:

Historical Overview: Discover the fascinating past of the Alaeddin Mosque, one of Konya's most important and ancient places of worship. Find more about its beginnings during the Seljuk era in the 12th century.

Architectural Features: Explore the mosque's distinctive architectural features, such as its soaring minaret, elaborate geometric patterns, and elaborate calligraphy. Find out how the Seljuk dynasty's artistic and cultural accomplishments are reflected in the mosque's design.

Spiritual Significance: Learn about the Alaeddin Mosque's religious significance as a place of prayer and reflection for Muslims in Konya. Discover the customs and ceremonies followed by mosque members, such as the Friday speeches and everyday prayers.

Konya Citadel:

Historical Context: Learn about the past of the Konya Citadel, a historic stronghold that has protected the city for many years. Examine its tactical significance as a defensive bastion throughout Konya's historical eras.

Architectural Highlights: Take in the citadel's striking walls, watchtowers, and bastions as you explore its architectural features. Discover the ingenuity and skill used in its construction, which has guaranteed its durability over time.

Cultural Legacy: Examine the Konya Citadel's cultural value as a representation of the city's tenacity and history. Discover how it has shaped Konya's identity and functioned as a hub for events and festivities in the community.

Modern-Day Relevance: Given that the citadel is still a well-liked landmark and popular tourist destination in Konya, consider its ongoing significance in the contemporary day. Find out how it has been refurbished and conserved to host festivals, exhibitions of historical artifacts, and cultural events.

Karatay Madrasa: A Jewel of Seljuk Architecture

Karatay Madrasa:

Historical Background: Learn about the beginnings of the magnificent Karatay Madrasa in the center of Konya, a prime example of Seljuk architecture. Find out about its construction in the thirteenth century, which was funded by the Seljuk Sultanate of Rum.

Architectural Marvel: Marvel at the architectural wonder and fine artistry of Karatay Madrasa, which is distinguished by its geometric patterns, elegant entrances, and gorgeous tilework. Find out how the artistic and cultural accomplishments of the Seljuk era are reflected in its design.

Educational Institution: Learn about Karatay Madrasa's function as a medieval hub for Islamic learning and research. Find more about the courses and instruction provided to students, including the sciences, Islamic law, and theology.

Cultural Heritage: Examine Karatay Madrasa's cultural value as a representation of Konya's illustrious past and cerebral history. See how, throughout its history, it has functioned as a center for spiritual enlightenment and intellectual interchange.

Preservation Efforts: Consider the continuous initiatives to maintain and safeguard Karatay Madrasa as a national heritage and architectural icon. Find more about the conservation and restoration efforts being undertaken to preserve its historical value and aesthetic appeal for future generations.

Ince Minaret Medrese: Witness to Konya's Cultural Heritage

Historical Background: Discover the Ince Minaret Medrese's lengthy past, which is evidence of Konya's rich cultural legacy. Learn about its beginnings in the Seljuk era in the 13th century, when the Seljuk Sultanate of Rum commissioned it.

Architectural Splendor: Admire the Ince Minaret Medrese's exquisite architecture, which is distinguished by its elaborate tilework, graceful minaret, and elaborate doorway. Discover the distinctive fusion of Islamic, Anatolian, and Seljuk architectural forms that make this historical site stand out.

Educational Institution: Learn about the Ince Minaret Medrese's original role as a hub for Islamic research and education. Find more about the courses that were available to students; the courses included a wide range of subjects, such as science, law, and theology.

Cultural Significance: Examine the Ince Minaret Medrese's cultural value as a representation of Konya's spiritual and intellectual legacy. Learn how, throughout its history, it has drawn researchers and students from all over the world by acting as a beacon of knowledge and enlightenment.

Preservation Efforts: Consider the continuous attempts to maintain and safeguard the Ince Minaret Medrese as an important cultural resource. Find out about the conservation and restoration efforts being undertaken to preserve its historical value and architectural integrity for future generations to enjoy.

Konya Archaeological Museum: Unveiling Ancient Treasures

Introduction to the Museum: Located in the center of Konya, the Konya Archaeological Museum is a treasure mine of historic relics and cultural items. Find more about its founding and goal to protect and promote the area's rich archeological heritage.

Ancient Anatolian Civilizations:
Take a trip back in time and explore relics from the Paleolithic to the Byzantine periods, spanning thousands of years. Discover the many civilizations that formerly flourished in Anatolia, such as the Greek, Lydian, Phrygian, and Hittite cultures.

Highlights of the Collection: Admire the museum's astounding assortment of items, which includes coins, jewelry, sculptures, and pottery. Explore famous items like the sarcophagi of the Phrygian kings and the Karun Treasure, an assemblage of Hellenistic gold and silver objects.

Islamic Art and Culture: Discover the rich legacy of Islamic art and culture in Konya, which includes beautiful calligraphy, illuminated manuscripts, and ornamental arts. Find out how the Mevlevi Order and Sufism influenced the artistic heritage of the area.

Interactive Exhibits and Educational Programs: Engage with multimedia installations and interactive displays that bring ancient history to life. Interactive exhibits and educational programs are also available. Take part in offerings that include informative seminars and expertly led tours by historians and archaeologists that shed light on Konya's interesting past.

Preservation and Conservation: Get knowledge about the museum's attempts to protect and preserve its priceless collection of antiquities for upcoming generations. Find out about the difficulties involved in preserving archeological artifacts and the methods employed to prevent the degradation of delicate items.

Consider the importance of the Konya Archaeological Museum as a cultural establishment devoted to conserving and honoring Anatolia's rich past. Examine how the displays deepen your understanding of Konya's historic treasures by illuminating the region's rich history and cultural tapestry.

Chapter 3: Immersing in Sufi Culture

Visiting Sufi Tekkes and Zawiyas: Sanctuaries of Spiritual Practice

Introduction to Sufi Retreats: Travel through the hallowed places known as tekkes and zawiyas as you embark on a spiritual adventure. Find out how important they are as hubs for group worship, meditation, and spiritual practice.

Historical Origins: Go back to the early days of Islam, when Sufi masters and pupils met in quiet places to practice spiritual reflection and devotion, to learn about the roots of Sufi tekkes and zawiyas. Learn how these retreats developed as hubs for Sufi communities over time.

Architectural Features: Be in awe of the Sufi tekkes and Zawiyas' exquisite simplicity and modest architecture, which are distinguished by their peaceful surroundings. Examine how these retreats are set up; they usually have prayer halls, meditation areas, and common areas for rituals and meetings.

Spiritual Practices: Get direct experience with the dhikr (remembrance of God), meditation, and recitation of Sufi poetry and scriptures that are practiced in Sufi tekkes and zawiyas. Take part in Sufi ceremonies and rituals to develop a sense of transcendence, inner serenity, and connectedness.

Guidance and Mentorship: Consult with seasoned Sufi masters who supervise tekkes and zawiya operations for advice and mentoring. Discover the spiritual practices and teachings that these knowledgeable mentors have to offer, which place a strong emphasis on achieving spiritual insight and heart purity.

Community and Fellowship: As you immerse yourself in the hospitable and inclusive atmosphere of tekkes and zawiyas, you'll have the opportunity to connect with other seekers and members of the Sufi community. Discover a profound sense of spiritual connection and belonging that surpasses social and cultural divides via a sense of togetherness and fraternity.

Consider the life-changing potential of traveling to Sufi tekkes and zawiyas, where seekers from all walks of life can receive inspiration, support, and guidance. Examine how, in a world that is changing all the time, these hallowed retreats nevertheless act as havens of serenity and enlightenment.

Meeting with Modern Sufi Practitioners

Introduction to Modern Sufism: Interact with modern Sufis, who continue the age-old traditions of inner transformation and spiritual enlightenment in the modern world. Discover the various backgrounds, ideologies, and customs of these people.

Encounters with Sufi Masters: Look for chances to have a meeting with contemporary Sufi masters and spiritual mentors who live out the values of wisdom, love, and compassion that their forebears advocated. Examine their teachings and perspectives on the Sufi path and the quest for heavenly closeness.

Discourses and Workshops: Participate in talks, seminars, and workshops conducted by contemporary Sufi practitioners to hear them share their insights and experiences with students and seekers. Examine subjects like the value of practicing spiritual discipline, developing inner virtues, and achieving spiritual realization.

Meditation and Contemplation: Engage in guided meditation sessions and contemplative practices led by contemporary Sufi practitioners. These practices give a space for introspection, self-awareness, and mindfulness. Discover the transforming potential of spiritual activities that clear the mind and make room for the divine to enter your heart.

Community Gatherings and Sufi Circles: Join contemporary Sufi practitioners in organizing Sufi circles and community events, where members assemble to partake in devotional activities, music, and poetry that draw inspiration from Sufi teachings. Savor the feeling of harmony and spiritual closeness that arises from gathering together for worship.

Service and Social Outreach: Investigate the humanitarian and social outreach projects carried out by contemporary Sufi practitioners, who are motivated by the values of social justice, service, and compassion. Find out about their endeavors to tackle societal problems and mitigate the agony of the poor, adhering to the teachings of Sufi saints and mystics.

Consider the enlightening experiences you had when you visited with contemporary Sufis, who exemplify the eternal principles and teachings of Sufism in current settings. Examine how seekers can be motivated to pursue inner peace and divine enlightenment on their spiritual path by their example, advice, and wisdom.

Sufi Music and Poetry: Delving into the Soulful Traditions of Konya

Introduction to Sufi Arts: Dive into the rich, deep traditions of Sufi poetry and music, which have long thrived in Konya. Examine how these artistic manifestations facilitate divine contact and spiritual transcendence.

Whirling Melodies and Mystical Lyrics: Soak in the hypnotic rhythms and eerie melodies that induce a feeling of spiritual ecstasy that defines Sufi music. Discover the ethereal words of Sufi poetry, which delve into themes of unity with the Beloved, divine love, and desire.

The Legacy of Rumi: Explore the deep impact of Rumi's poetry and music on Konya's cultural landscape in "The Legacy of Rumi." Discover how his classic poems, "Divan-e Shams-e Tabrizi" and

"Mathnawi," have influenced poets, musicians, and truth-seekers worldwide.

Qawwali and Sema Performances: Take in Sema and Qawwali concerts in Konya, where Sufi musicians and dervishes unite to honor the divine with song and dance. Discover the transforming power of these holy rites that raise consciousness to higher planes and awaken the soul.

Poetry Readings and Literary Salons: Take part in Konya's poetry and Sufi literature-focused literary salons and poetry readings. Interact with well-known poets and academics who discuss the spiritual meaning and lyrical elegance of Sufi poetry to develop a greater understanding of the mystical Sufi traditions.

Sufi Music Workshops and Retreats: Participate in seminars and retreats on Sufi music hosted by local professors and artists in Konya. Discover how to develop a closer relationship with the holy via musical expression and spiritual practice, as well as learn about the traditional instruments and musical approaches utilized in Sufi music.

Consider the enormous influence that Sufi poetry and music have had on Konya's spiritual legacy and sense of cultural identity. Examine how these spiritual traditions continue to uplift and inspire the hearts of both believers and non-believers, encouraging harmony and unity in the search for divine truth and beauty.

Chapter 4: Culinary Delights and Local Flavors

Exploring Konya's Traditional Cuisine: From Mevlana Kebab to Etli Ekmek

Introduction to Konyan Cuisine: Savor the rich history and wide range of flavors found in Konya's traditional cuisine as you go on a gastronomic journey. Learn how the city's physical position, historical influences, and cultural diversity have affected its culinary traditions.

Mevlana Kebab: Savor the famous Mevlana Kebab, a tasty treat named for the well-known Sufi mystic Rumi. Discover the special way this dish is made, which includes soft meat skewers that are perfectly grilled and seasoned with flavorful spices.

Etli Ekmek: Savor the earthy tones of this classic Anatolian flatbread topped with spices, onions, and minced meat. Savor the filling taste of this popular street meal that has been a favorite among Kenyans for many years.

Yaprak Sarma: Savor the subtle aromas of Yaprak Sarma, which is made of grains, herbs, and spices filled inside vine leaves. Discover the cultural importance of this dish, which is frequently served during Konya's family get-togethers and celebrations.

Fırın Kebabı: Savor the rich and flavorful Fırın Kebabı, a meal of slow-cooked beef or lamb stewed in a tasty sauce with a tomato basis. Learn the traditional method of making this filling stew in clay pots and serving it with warm, freshly baked bread.

Beyran Soup: Treat yourself to a warm bowl of this robust soup made with rice and lamb that is flavored with saffron and cinnamon, among other aromatic spices. Discover the roots of this popular comfort food, which dates back to the Seljuk era.

Desserts and Sweets: Satisfy your sweet craving with a variety of traditional Konyan desserts, like Güllaç (milk pudding infused with rosewater), Baklava (layered pastry with almonds and syrup), and Şekerpare (sweet semolina cookies). Savor the subtle textures and enticing sweetness of these delicious delicacies.

Consider the distinct flavors that define Konya's culinary heritage as well as the culinary joys of the region's traditional cuisine. Examine how food fosters a sense of shared identity and cultural pride, uniting people to celebrate the diverse range of Anatolian customs and flavors.

Tea Gardens and Turkish Delights: Sampling Konya's Sweet Side

Introduction to Tea Gardens: Take in the tranquil atmosphere of traditional Turkish tea gardens as you start your exploration of Konya's sweet side. Find out how these quaint outdoor areas offer the ideal environment for unwinding, mingling, and indulging in delectable delights.

Turkish Tea: Enjoy a hot cup of this popular beverage, which is adored by both residents and tourists. Discover the art of tea culture in Turkey, where making and serving tea is seen as a gesture of kindness and welcome.

Assorted Turkish Delights: Treat yourself to a variety of Turkish sweets, also known as "lokum," which is a confection of sugar, flour, and different flavorings including citrus, pistachios, and rosewater. Savor the delicate textures and melt-in-your-mouth sweetness of these traditional Turkish sweets.

Baklava: Enjoy the richness that is just seductive in baklava, a pastry filled with chopped nuts and sweetened with honey or syrup that is constructed from layers of thin phyllo dough. Learn the skill and technique that go into making this well-liked delicacy, which is typically consumed with a steaming cup of tea.

Sütlaç: Treat yourself to a cool bowl of sütlaç, a creamy rice pudding infused with vanilla and cinnamon for flavor. Savor the comforting sweetness and creamy texture of this classic Turkish dessert, which is typically served cold and topped with toasted nuts.

Kunefe: This delicious dessert, which is formed of shredded phyllo dough covered with sweet cheese and drenched in syrup, will wow your taste buds with its distinct flavors. Discover the delectable blend of crunchy, oozy, and syrupy textures that make Kunefe a beloved treat in Konya.

Consider how pleasant it was to encounter Konya's sweet side, where Turkish sweets and tea gardens combine to produce happy, restful, and gastronomic moments. Discover how the rich cultural legacy and culinary traditions of Turkey are reflected in these classic sweets that leave a lasting impression on everyone who indulges in their sweetness.

Culinary Workshops and Food Tours: A Tasty Adventure Awaits

Introduction to Culinary Workshops: Take part in immersive culinary classes and food tours to start your culinary adventure around Konya.

Find out how these encounters provide a practical way to learn about the traditional cooking methods and rich culinary legacy of Konya.

Traditional Cooking Classes: Take a culinary lesson taught by local chefs and culinary experts, then get your hands dirty and explore the world of Konyan food. Discover how to make traditional meals like yaprak sarma, etli ekmek, and Mevlana kebab using ingredients that are procured locally and freshly.

Artisanal Food Production: Discover the methods used in Konya's artisanal food manufacturing, which shape the city's culinary scene. Learn about the procurement and preparation of essential components used in traditional Konyan meals by visiting the local markets, bakeries, and spice shops.

Farm-to-Table Experiences: Savor the abundant vegetables and seasonal treats of Konya while reconnecting with the region's agricultural legacy through farm-to-table experiences. Take part in events like grape harvesting, olive oil tastings, and farm tours to develop a greater understanding of the contribution of agriculture to Konya's culinary traditions.

Street Food Tours: Take a mouthwatering tour of Konya's lively districts and bustling bazaars while sampling local cuisine. Explore the city's culinary hotspots and sample a wide range of street food delicacies, such as aromatic kahve (Turkish coffee), crispy simit (bread rings with sesame seeds), and savory gözleme (stuffed flatbread).

Dessert Making Workshops: Satisfy your sweet craving with classes that highlight Konya's exquisite sweets' artistry and workmanship. Learn the techniques needed to make these delectable desserts, including baklava, şekerpare, and güllaç, under the direction of experienced pastry chefs.

Consider the wonderful meals you had and the newfound culinary abilities you learned while in Konya. Discover how Konya's thriving culinary industry is defined by the rich tapestry of flavors, scents, and traditions that can be experienced through these immersive seminars and food tours.

Chapter 5: Off the Beaten Path

Day Trips from Konya: Discovering Nearby Gems

Cappadocia: Travel to Cappadocia and experience its enchanted scenery, which includes fairy chimneys, historic caves, and wacky rock formations. Take in the breathtaking views of Göreme National Park, visit the underground cities of Derinkuyu and Kaymaklı, and experience a sunrise hot air balloon trip over the surreal scenery.

Pamukkale: Discover the natural beauties of Pamukkale, a place renowned for its thermal springs and travertine terraces. Take a tour of the pristine white terraces of the ancient city of Hierapolis and plunge into the warm, mineral-rich waters, which are said to have therapeutic qualities.

Antalya: Take a vacation to the idyllic Mediterranean city of Antalya, where you can explore historic monuments, beautiful beaches, and turquoise waters. Discover the historic sites of Perge and Aspendos, meander through the quaint lanes of the historic center, and unwind on the sunny beaches of Konyaaltı and Lara.

Karahöyük: Just a short drive from Konya, explore the ancient site of Karahöyük. Discover the 3rd millennium BCE Hittite settlement's ancient ruins and be amazed by the remarkably preserved artifacts and colossal constructions that archaeologists have found.

Sille: Tucked away in the gorgeous countryside close to Konya, the charming village of Sille will transport you back in time.

Discover its storied cathedrals, monasteries, and homes from the Ottoman era. You can also take strolls down the serene alleys that are bordered by old stone structures and mulberry trees.

Beyşehir Lake: Take a leisurely day excursion to Turkey's largest freshwater lake, Beyşehir Lake, to escape the bustle of the city. Savor leisurely boat rides, lakeside picnics, and bird watching excursions while immersed in the pure beauty and calm of nature.

Consider the wide range of day trip alternatives that are accessible from Konya, each of which offers a special fusion of historical interest, cultural richness, and natural beauty. Discover how these local treasures offer the ideal chance to get away from the city and take in the splendors of Turkey's varied scenery and rich cultural legacy.

Rural Konya: Experiencing Village Life and Rural Hospitality

Introduction to Rural Konya: Discover the allure and ease of rural living in Konya's countryside by venturing off the well-traveled route. Explore the pristine beauty of the Turkish countryside and experience the warmth and welcome of local communities.

Village Homestays: Spend a night or two in one of Konya's rural communities to get a firsthand look at real village life. Discover the customs and rhythms of rural life by staying with local families and taking part in everyday activities including farming, cooking, and traditional crafts.

Agricultural Tours: Take an agricultural tour through the lush farmlands of Konya to learn about the customs of the local farmers and take part in seasonal tasks like planting, harvesting, and crop-tending. Savor the flavors of freshly harvested vegetables and handcrafted treats while seeing organic farms, wineries, and olive groves.

Countryside Walks: Take strolls along hiking routes that meander through aromatic orchards, lush valleys, and rolling hills to discover the scenic splendor of Konya's countryside. Along the route, you'll come across quaint towns, historic ruins, and expansive views that provide a window into the rich natural and cultural history of the area.

Village Markets and Festivals: Learn about the colorful village markets and celebrations that unite rural communities in honor of their cultural heritage. Explore booths offering regional produce, handicrafts, and artisanal products while taking in the vibrant ambiance of folklore, music, and dancing.

Culinary Experiences: Savor farm-to-table gastronomic adventures that highlight the tastes and products of rural Konya. Take cooking lessons from neighborhood chefs, learn how to make classic village fare with in-season, fresh ingredients, and savor farm-fresh meals lovingly prepared by your kind hosts.

Consider the enriching experiences you had while experiencing rural hospitality and village life in Konya, where the natural beauty of the area combined with the friendliness of the locals makes for enduring ties and wonderful memories. Examine how a greater understanding of the timeless customs and straightforward pleasures of rural Turkey can be gained from these genuine interactions.

Eco-Tourism Initiatives: Connecting with Nature in Konya's Surroundings

Introduction to Ecotourism: Experience the natural beauty and richness of Konya's environs by engaging in eco-tourism projects that take you on a voyage of exploration and discovery. Find out how these programs encourage environmentally conscious travel and strengthen ties to the natural world.

National Parks and Nature Reserves: Hiking, birdwatching, and wildlife observation are all possible in Konya's national parks and nature reserves. Discover the region's many ecosystems. Explore the wild topography of Akşehir Canyon, the serene serenity of Beyşehir Lake, and the breathtaking scenery of Sultan Marshes National Park.

Guided Nature Walks: Take part in guided nature walks with knowledgeable park rangers and naturalists to learn about the plants and animals of Konya's wilderness areas. Find out about the distinctive ecosystems in the area, conservation initiatives, and the significance of protecting biodiversity for upcoming generations.

Birdwatching Expeditions: Take part in bird watching excursions to witness the abundant variety of birds inhabiting Konya's marshes, woodlands, and grasslands. Visit Sultan Marshes to observe migrating birds like flamingos, pelicans, and cranes, or look for native species like saker falcons and white-headed ducks in their native environments.

Cycling and Adventure Tours: Get off the beaten path and into the heart of nature with cycling and adventure excursions, which will show you the beauty of Konya's countryside. Riding a bike over rolling hills, lush valleys, and aromatic orchards, discover picturesque routes, isolated communities, and undiscovered treasures.

Community-Based Tourism: Participate in community-based tourism programs that foster sustainable development and cross-cultural exchange. Enjoy locally produced food, stay in eco-friendly lodging, and take part in customary events like storytelling sessions, folk dances, and handicraft workshops.

Contemplate the revolutionary potential of ecotourism endeavors in Konya, providing chances for visitors to reestablish a connection with the natural world, bolster local economies, and aid in the preservation of the area's ecological and cultural legacy. Examine how these immersive experiences help visitors and the environment alike by fostering greater awareness of the diversity and beauty of Konya's surroundings.

Chapter 6: Practical Information

Getting to Konya: Transportation Options

By Air: From major Turkish cities including Istanbul, Ankara, and Izmir, domestic flights are available to Konya Airport (KYA), where you can arrive. International passengers can also arrive in Konya using connecting flights from Ankara or Istanbul.

By Train: Make use of Turkey's vast rail network to take a train to Konya. High-speed trains (YHT) from Ankara and Istanbul provide direct links to the city all day long. Travel through the picturesque and comfortable Anatolian countryside on air-conditioned trains that are modern and air-conditioned.

By Bus: Istanbul, Ankara, Antalya, and Izmir are just a few of the major Turkish cities from which you may take an interstate bus to Konya. Many bus companies provide regular, reasonably priced transportation to Konya, making it an easy choice for tourists. Konya's bus stations are well-appointed with facilities like ticket booths, cafes, and waiting places.

By Car: Konya may be reached by car via Turkey's well-kept road system, which links the city to important routes like the E90 and E96. Experience the liberty and adaptability of traveling at your speed through the Turkish countryside, where beautiful roadways provide stunning vistas of undulating hills, verdant valleys, and important historical sites.

Local Transportation: Take one of Konya's many public transit choices, including buses, trams, and taxis, to get around the city center and neighboring areas. Travelers may conveniently experience Konya's cultural and historical riches thanks to the city's dependable and efficient public transportation system, which makes it easy to get to neighborhoods, suburbs, and major attractions.

Turkey's sophisticated transportation system makes traveling to Konya simple and convenient, regardless of your mode of transportation of choice you can drive your car, take the train, take a bus, or fly. Examine the variety of options available and select the form of transportation that best fits your schedule and travel preferences.

Where to Stay: Accommodation Recommendations

Luxury Hotels:

Rumi Hotel: Located in the center of Konya's historic district, the Rumi Hotel invites you to indulge in luxury. Savor sophisticated accommodations, including suites and rooms, excellent dining options, and flawless service all conveniently located close to popular sites like the Alaeddin Mosque and Mevlana Museum.

Hilton Garden Inn Konya: With chic accommodations, a rooftop restaurant with panoramic views, and several amenities like a fitness facility and business centers, this hotel offers contemporary luxury and convenience.

Boutique Hotels:

Anemon Hotel Konya: Nestled in a historic structure, this boutique-style hotel offers exquisite décor and individualized service. Savor Turkish cuisine at the hotel's restaurant, unwind in comfortable accommodations, and visit neighboring sites like the İnce Minaret Museum and Karatay Madrasa.

Neva Hotel: Take in the peace in this boutique hotel with nice rooms, a lovely courtyard garden, and a small café that serves pastries and Turkish coffee. Its central location makes it simple to get to restaurants, shops, and historical sites.

Budget Accommodations:

Otel Selçuk: Take advantage of inexpensive comfort at this welcoming hotel with tidy, comfortable rooms, free breakfast, and helpful staff. Situated near Konya's primary tourist destinations and public transport hubs, this budget-friendly option is perfect for tourists.

Konya Dervish Hotel: Enjoy traditional Turkish hospitality at this affordable hotel, which features basic but comfortable rooms, a typical Turkish breakfast buffet, and a prime position near Mevlana Square and the Mevlana Museum.

Guesthouses and Homestays:

Sillehan Hotel: The historic village of Sille is home to the guesthouse known as the Sillehan Hotel, where you may experience the allure of village life. Enjoy home-cooked meals made with ingredients that are sourced locally, stay in charming rooms decorated with traditional Turkish décor, and see the village's old churches and monasteries.

Ahi Evran Guesthouse: This family-run homestay offers cozy lodging, freshly prepared meals, and attentive service. Come experience true Turkish hospitality here. Situated in a serene community, it offers a tranquil haven from the cacophony of urban life.

Hostels:

Konya Hostel: For a low cost, stay in the center of Konya at Konya Hostel, which provides dormitory-style lodging, shared amenities, and a welcoming environment. Ideal for independent travelers and backpackers who want to meet other adventurers and have an affordable exploration of Konya.

Essential Tips for Travelers: Cultural Etiquette and Safety Guidelines

Respect Local Customs and Traditions:

. When entering mosques and places of worship, dress modestly by covering your arms, legs, and shoulders.

. Be considerate of religious customs and practices and take off your shoes before entering homes and mosques.

. Say "Merhaba" (Hello) or "Selamün Aleyküm" (Peace be upon you) to the locals and smile.

Cultural Sensitivity:

. Refrain from making public shows of affection since in conservative environments, it could be deemed improper.

. Avoid taking pictures of people without their consent, particularly when you're in a remote place.

. Respect religious customs and beliefs, such as keeping a fast during Ramadan and going to Friday prayers.

Safety Precautions:

. Be on the lookout for pickpockets in busy places and on public transit, and keep your belongings safe.

. Remain aware of any potential threats and local safety advice, particularly if you are going to be in rural areas or close to the Syrian border.

. Make use of reliable transportation options and stay away from nighttime alone, especially when visiting new places.

Health and Hygiene:

. In rural areas especially, stay away from gastrointestinal problems by drinking purified or bottled water.

. To prevent infection, carry hand sanitizer with you and maintain excellent hygiene, which includes frequent handwashing.

. Make sure you have travel insurance that covers medical emergencies and bring the required drugs.

Language Barrier:

. To help with communication, pick up some simple Turkish phrases or carry a phrasebook with you.

. When speaking with those who may not speak English well, use plain language or, if needed, translation applications. Also, be patient and courteous.

Currency and Payments:

.Keep a variety of cash and credit/debit cards on you in case some businesses, particularly in rural areas, do not accept cards.

. To avoid fraud, familiarize yourself with the local currency, the Turkish Lira, and exchange money at banks or authorized exchange bureaus.

Emergency Contacts:

. Maintain a list of emergency contacts that includes the contact information for your lodging, the local authorities, and any embassy or consulates.

. Put emergency numbers into your phone, such as 155 for police help and 112 for general emergencies.

Conclusion

Embracing the Sufi Soul of Konya: Reflections on a Mystical Journey

The deep influence of Konya's Sufi history on my spirit strikes me as I think back on my trip across the city. I was overcome with a feeling of calm, peace, and spiritual resonance as soon as I stepped foot in this historic city, and it pervaded every part of my experience.

I could feel the echoes of bygone eras as I meandered through the winding lanes of Konya's old town, where seekers of enlightenment and divine love are still motivated by the teachings of Rumi and the mystics of the Mevlevi Order. Mosques, madrasas, and mausoleums around the city invited me to stop, think, and commune with Sufism's ageless knowledge, acting as sacred checkpoints along my journey.

I was enthralled with the tranquility of Rumi's last resting place, where pilgrims from all over the world congregate to honor the great poet and mystic when I visited the Mevlana Museum. Seeing the captivating Sema ritual, with its whirling dervishes spinning in the ecstasy of devotion, took me to a world beyond ordinary perception, where dance, music, and meditation come together to awaken the spirit.

I had significant epiphanies and moments of insight while learning about Konya's rich cultural past, which helped me better comprehend the worldwide Sufi message of love, harmony, and spiritual awakening. I had a strong sense of kinship and belonging with the people of Konya, whether it was by indulging in the tastes of regional cuisine, interacting with artists and musicians, or just taking in the warmth of human connection.

I leave this beautiful city with a fresh sense of motivation and purpose, knowing that the Sufi spirit will follow me and continue to light my path long after I've left. Konya is a location where the eternal dance of love is revealed in every heartbeat, breath, and stride down the path of mystic revelation. It is not just a destination; it is a sanctuary for the soul.

Appendix

Glossary of Sufi Terms

Sufism: The mystic subset of Islam that concentrated on achieving enlightenment and inner knowledge via devotion to the Divine, dhikr (remembering God), and meditation.

Dhikr: The spiritual practice of remembering God's names or characteristics aloud and cleansing one's heart through repetition.

Tariqa: A Sufi order or spiritual path that aids seekers in achieving spiritual realization through a particular set of teachings, practices, and ceremonies led by a spiritual master (sheik).

Sheikh: A sheik is a spiritual guide or instructor of a Sufi order who is esteemed for their knowledge, discernment, and proficiency in Sufi doctrine and practice.

Mureed: A Sufi sheik's disciple or follower who is dedicated to the tariqa spiritual path and is mentored by them on their quest for enlightenment.

Majlis: An assembly or meeting of Sufis for group meditation, spiritual discussion, and collective devotion; usually presided over by a sheikh or other senior member of the Sufi community.

Zikr: Another word for dhikr, meaning remembering and calling upon the name of God as a means of spiritual cleansing and devotion.

Maktubat: A Sufi master's collected letters or correspondence with their disciples and followers, providing lessons, advice, and spiritual insights.

Fana: The extinction of the ego (nafs) in the Divine Presence, which is seen as a crucial phase in the Sufi's spiritual path towards oneness with God (maqam al-tawhid).

Baqa: The afterglow of fana, in which the Sufi unites with the Divine while maintaining consciousness of their own identity, is the state of subsistence or eternal being in God.

Haqiqa: The ultimate reality or truth of existence, which transcends ordinary knowledge and perception and is known via direct spiritual experience and realization.

Marifat: Gnosis or spiritual knowledge gained by firsthand encounters with the Divine that results in a greater understanding of life's mysteries and the essence of reality.

Majzub: A Sufi mystic who is so consumed by heavenly love that they lose awareness of the outside world; they frequently behave strangely or experience ecstasies.

Maqam: On the Sufi path, a spiritual station or level of attainment that symbolizes phases of spiritual development and realization leading to unity with God.

Qutb: The universe's spiritual axis or pole, revered by Sufis as a saintly figure with exceptional spiritual grace and authority who upholds cosmic order and leads humanity towards enlightenment.

Useful Phrases in Turkish

Greetings:
Hello: Merhaba
Good morning: Günaydın
Good afternoon: İyi öğlen
Good evening: İyi akşamlar
Goodbye: Hoşça kal
Polite Expressions:
Please: Lütfen
Thank you: Teşekkür ederim
You're welcome: Rica ederim
Excuse me: Affedersiniz
I'm sorry: Üzgünüm
Basic Conversational Phrases:

Yes: Evet
No: Hayır
What is your name?: Adınız ne?
My name is...: Benim adım...
How are you?: Nasılsınız?
I'm fine, thank you: İyiyim, teşekkür ederim
Directions:
Where is...?: ...nerede?
Go straight: Düz git
Turn left/right: Sola/sağa dön
Is it far?: Uzak mı?
Eating and Drinking:
I would like...: ...istemek istiyorum
Water: Su
Food: Yemek
Tea: Çay
Coffee: Kahve
Delicious: Lezzetli
Cheers!: Şerefe!
Numbers:
One: Bir
Two: İki

Three: Üç
Four: Dört
Five: Beş

Common Courtesies:

May I help you?: Size yardımcı olabilir miyim?

Have a nice day!: İyi günler!

Enjoy your meal!: Afiyet olsun!

Congratulations!: Tebrikler!

Good luck!: İyi şanslar!

Emergency Phrases:

Help!: Yardım!

Fire!: Yangın!

Police!: Polis!

Doctor!: Doktor!

I need help: Yardıma ihtiyacım var

When visiting Turkey, don't forget to practice these words to improve your ability to communicate!

Final Thoughts and Recommendations for Saying Goodbye to Konya

Consider the deep insights and memories you have gained from your stay in this magical city as you get ready to say goodbye to Konya. Here are some closing ideas and suggestions for bidding Konya farewell:

Reflect on Your Journey: Give yourself some time to consider the sights, sounds, and experiences that have moved you during your travels through Konya. To gain a deeper understanding and appreciation of the spiritual heritage of the city, think about journaling or practicing meditation on your experiences.

Visit Your Favorite Spots: Make one final trip back to your favorite Konya locations before you depart. Savor the moments and treasure the memories you've made, whether they be in the quiet surroundings of Beyşehir Lake, the busy bazaars of the old town, or the tranquil gardens of the Mevlana Museum.

Say Goodbye with Gratitude: Give thanks to everyone you've encountered along the way, including the amiable locals, the informed tour guides, and the kind hosts who have greeted you with open arms. Tell them how much your warmth has meant to you and express your gratitude for their hospitality and kindness.

Leave a Positive Impact: As you get ready to go, think about how you can positively influence Konya and the local community. Buy handcrafted trinkets from local artists, shop at family-run establishments, and think about contributing to groups that protect Konya's cultural legacy as ways to show your support.

Promise to Return: Bid farewell to Konya with a sincere intention to come back at some point. Tell Konya that you have a special place in your heart for it and that you will always carry its spirit with you wherever you travel, whether it's to further your spiritual development, reunite with friends you've made, or just to experience the wonder of this enchanted city.

May the recollections of Konya's Sufi soul uplift and inspire you as you travel on, directing you toward a deeper comprehension, compassion, and inner peace. Konya, hoşça kal until we cross paths again.

Printed in Great Britain
by Amazon